AFTER PUBLISHING

Self–Publish and Get Results
Like a Major Publisher

Editor: Yaron Ginsberg

Cover design and page layout: Lazar Kackarovski

Proof editor: Louisa Jordan

Library of Congress Cataloging-in-Publication data available.

ISBN: 978-1-938591-68-6

eISBN: 978-1-938591-69-3

Published by Sole Books, Beverly Hills, California

Printed in the United States of America

www.solebooks.com

AFTER PUBLISHING

Self–Publish and Get Results
Like a Major Publisher

Steve Berg

Sole
BOOKS

Table of Contents

AUTHOR'S NOTE:

This book isn't about writing or authoring a book.

This book isn't about how to manipulate bestseller rankings and accumulate false reviews.

This book is about reaching readers, growing your readership, and building your author brand using proven methods.

It's about creating effective, results-oriented campaigns.

It's about selling your book in dozens of languages worldwide.

AND LASTLY:

There are many guides and courses about the mechanics of placing an ad on Facebook, Amazon, or Google. This is not what this book is about.

It's about articulating the most effective message about your books, finding readers, and making them want to read your book.

THE MICROPUBLISHER REVOLUTION IS HERE TO STAY, AND YOU ARE IT

Over the last decade, the publishing industry has gone through rapid changes. A revolution that is shaking and shaping the industry much like the one that shaped the music industry. The lines between a big publisher and a micropublisher, between local and global, have become invisible.

This is the age of the micropublisher. We believe that the title micropublisher (as opposed to self–published author) is the right title for millions of authors who take the mantel and the responsibilities of a professional publisher.

We, a husband and wife team based in Los Angeles, have built a global micropublishing business with almost no overhead by utilizing available tools—most of them free. In this book, we will demonstrate how you can do it too, from the comfort of your home. Bring your book to readers all over the world in dozens of languages using proven methods.

Widening your scope from local to global can contribute significantly to your author brand and to your books' sales and it should be an integral part of your journey. This is exactly what we've learned from our journey. You can be a micropublisher working from home and get results like a major publisher. Here's how.

CHAPTER 1
Stay Small—Win Big

For the last five years, we were selling our books all over the world from the comfort of our home. From the outset, we described ourselves as a *living room publisher*.

We started by working out a few principles describing how we would like to see our business grow, and launched our first book. The success of *The Flea—The Amazing Story of Leo Messi* started it all.

Our books have grossed millions of dollars so far and continue to sell as we write this book, and it is clear to us that our model could come in handy for many micropublishers everywhere.

Each journey is different. Ours started from the end. We first tried to define our readers. Once we answered this question, we went all the way back to the drawing board. We outlined ideas about the books we wanted to publish that would cater to what our readers would have wanted to read. Once we established the reader's profile and the book's profile, we set up a plan. This is not to say that you should do this before you write your book. Writing a book—especially fiction—is a personal and artistic endeavor and you shouldn't impose marketing concerns on your writing process. But when you decide to self-publish your book, you must change hats. Out goes the writer, in goes the publisher. And the publisher's task is to produce the book (the *product*), market it to the reader (the *customer*), and make a sale.

As a publisher, you have to conceptualize this process. You can do it after you finish writing, when the book is ready to upload or print, and you can do it before you write the first word. And in case your book fails to reach readers, you shouldn't give up. Pivot, start again, and you may find success.

This is something most established publisher won't do. They will throw a book on the wall and if it doesn't stick, they'll move on. This is *their* business model. But because it is *your book,* you can try again and again until you find success. You'll do things no publisher will do for your book. Because you care, and because you can.

As a writer and a publisher, you should have the two "personalities" coexist harmoniously within you in order to get the best results. Therefore, the key question you should ask yourself is: "What is right for me?"

We decided to stay small and think big. Remain a micropublisher but think like *Random House.* For us, staying small was a lifestyle decision, and it meant that we had to operate in a way that would be suitable for us. Our goals were: maintain minimal overhead, make minimal investments, and stay small while letting our books grow to their maximum potential.

As publishers, we had to define two essential principals regarding the market: We looked for a targeted niche with great growth potential for years to come, and we wanted this niche to be global.

But how should we reach out to the world?

The book industry has plenty of markets and fairs. We visited the Frankfurt Book Fair, the biggest book fair in the world, where business is conducted by meeting peers at the market floor. However, it was clear that being a micropublisher in the digital age was an advantage so great that there was no real need to hop on a plane for the Frankfurt or London Fairs.

We believed that publishing our books all over the world could be done from everywhere, provided we had a reliable internet connection. We weighed the risk and reward and concluded that if we were to fail, the financial ramifications would be minimal.

But if we were to succeed, it would open a whole new world of opportunities.

It all begins with taking control of the entire publishing process, especially the most challenging part: the post-publishing phase.

We started this phase before the first word was written. We were looking at sports biographies. We further looked at soccer biographies. We thought about a young demographic. We identified a niche. We started to plan our campaign by answering the following questions:

1. Is there a market?
2. Is there interest?
3. Where is the market?
4. Who are the competitors?
5. What is our advantage?
6. What is our USP (Unique Sale Point)?
7. What is our MUQ (Most Unique Quality)
8. Who are the customers?
9. What is the point of entry?
10. What is the time to market?
11. What is the required investment?
12. What would be a desirable outcome?

Watching our three kids grow up in LA, playing soccer from an early age, and being a family that was soccer-crazy, we noticed that the interest in soccer in the US was growing rapidly, and we knew that it was by far the most loved sport in the world.

Soccer books!

We answered the first three questions: There was interest, there was a market, and the market was global.

After examining the market, we realized that our advantage was the lack of well-written books about the biggest stars in the sport. The competition was scarce, and the quality was mediocre, at best. Our USP (Unique Sale Point) was the unique content and style of the books. We targeted children aged 9–14 and their soccer–loving parents and grandparents as our buyers.

Next, we looked for a point of entry, which was the international market, rather than the US. We budgeted the cost of bringing our first book to the market. At that point, we realized that most of the investment would be spent on post–publishing: advertising and marketing.

We decided that our first book would be about the best player of our time: Leo Messi. The interest in him was sky high all over the world. We researched, developed, and wrote the first book in the series: *The Flea—The Amazing Story of Leo Messi*, written by Michael Part. Messi's coming–of–age story had all the ingredients of a great novel. We felt that kids around the world would connect and respond to the book.

From a timing perspective, we needed 2 months to prep and produce the book, and the spring of 2013 was right. The publication date, our point of entry, was August 2013. We thought that we should launch in one of the weakest periods of book sales with less competition and be picked up during the fourth quarter and the holiday season.

When we broke down the budget, we came to the conclusion that developing, producing, and marketing the book in the US could be offset with selling translation rights first. We concluded that the advances from foreign rights sales would finance publishing and post–publishing costs in the US.

We had a plan. In the spring of 2013, we began to execute it.

IT IS NEVER TOO EARLY TO GO GLOBAL

We reached out to the world before our first copy was printed. Immediately after completing the print–ready PDF, we announced to nearly 1,000 publishers around the world that our new book's translation rights were available. Two days later, we received a request for a PDF from a Danish publisher, followed by requests from Japan and the UK. A couple of weeks later, we were already negotiating our first deals with several publishers from countries around the globe. These advances funded our publishing expenses in the US and ultimately funded a new micropublisher: Sole Books.

The investment of our post–publishing global launch was $60, which paid for a mail marketing service.

We published the book in the US in the summer of 2013. Five years later, the book still holds top spots in the soccer biographies category in the US and elsewhere, most of the time at the number one spot. It's been sold in 36 countries worldwide and laid the global groundwork for an ongoing series about the world's biggest soccer stars as well as other books we'd publish later.

HOW OUR EXPERIENCE APPLIES TO YOU

Choose the model that is right for you: In this day and age, the big and the small go hand in hand. You can choose how small or how big you would like to be and still get great results. No one can guarantee success. And it's harder for an outsider to define what success means for you. You might find it worthwhile to spend some time thinking about your goals as a micropublisher. But have no doubt: you can go to great lengths and stay small in operation, cost, and risk.

There is no publishing without post–publishing: The post–publishing process is overlooked by many self–published authors because it's challenging and perhaps not as "fun" as writing and producing a book. This is where you leave your comfort zone as an author and enter the world of marketing and sales. You should master it.

Realize what it takes: While taking your first steps in reaching readers, familiarize yourself with the ones you don't have yet. *Post–publishing* is probably the most challenging phase facing every author and publisher. You have to determine how much of your time and resources you are willing to contribute. When you don't have the knowhow or the organization that established publishers do, you need to compensate with commitment, creativity, and passion.

Go global from the get-go: Going global will enable you not only to sell many more books, it will give you the flexibility to find success in other markets if things won't go your way on your own.

Whether you are a self-published author or a micropublisher, opening your offerings to the world will multiply the chances that your books will be exposed and sold to more readers. When you look beyond your own language and market, you might strike gold. It feels great when you're reading a rave review about your work coming from a reader in another country. The moment when you receive a package with a few copies of your book in Swedish, Japanese, or Italian is priceless. And it feels even better when you get a wire transfer of royalties to your bank account.

But first, let's start with the first steps in your post-publishing process.

Like most SPs, you ask yourself, *how can I focus on my writing while actively keeping busy with post-publishing tasks of my finished book?* And if you are ready to do it, you might wonder, what is the most effective way I can promote and engage my would-be readers? How can I use available tools for promotion and marketing? What should I do to make effective decisions in areas beyond my area of expertise, especially those outside my comfort zone?

We asked ourselves these exact same questions and we chose to tackle them because we believed that it was the only way to do it right and take control. If we succeeded, so can you. This is our story. We hope it'll inspire you. Now it's your turn.

CHAPTER 2

No One Will Sell Your Book Better Than You!

We put together a list of keys which helped us establish our post–publishing work. We found these to be essential first steps.

KEY 1: DEFINE YOUR GOALS AND OBJECTIVES

Your unique goals and expectations will determine the rest of your journey.

Even if you are focused on one book, you must make a decision on whether this is a hobby or a business and make a list of your goals and objectives. For example:

- I don't care about earning money. I just want my book to be read.
- I would like to sell as many copies of my book as possible.
- I would like to be read and reviewed, get recognition, and build awareness for myself and my book regardless of the amount of sales.
- I just want to recover my publishing costs.
- I'd like to make a living as a self–published author.
- I would like to create a foundation for a series and build my author brand.

- I would like to become a micropublisher who publishes other authors.

Setting one or more of these goals will guide you in making critical decisions, give you a better understanding of the nature of your publishing endeavors, and help you clarify what it takes to achieve your goals.

KEY 2: DETACH YOURSELF FROM YOUR BOOK

Take a step back and think about your book, your readers, and your "writer identity" from an objective and analytical perspective.

Transform the imaginary reader you might have had in your mind while writing your book into an analytical customer profile. The more detailed and accurate the profile is, the more focused and targeted your post–publishing efforts will become.

Take a detached view of your book. A useful way to start this process is to write a coverage of your own book as if you are an editor or an agent reviewing a blind submission. This will give you the opportunity to evaluate your own work from a professional perspective. Try to figure out a way to honestly describe your book's pros and cons as though you are an editor who submits it to your editorial board for consideration. Make the case for the book. Suggest ideas to the marketing department. Try to evaluate whether the book could be sold globally. Analyze the financial prospects of the book, and whether it could cover the cost of production and marketing and when it'll turn a profit. It's a great practical exercise in which you detach from your "author self" and transform into your "publisher self."

KEY 3: TREAT IT AS A BUSINESS

Darren Hardy, the UK manager of Amazon's Kindle Direct Publishing, described the choice any self–published author should make: "Treat it [publishing] as a business and treat it seriously if you want to make a big impact. If you are serious about trying to become a bestseller [author] in however you choose to define that, then it's going to take some work. So, you need to think about how that's going to happen. You can't just publish the book and then sit back and think, 'Great, I'll now wait and then next week I will be at Number One and an International Bestseller.' So, if they're the kinds of things you're aiming for, then think about the plan. Put a plan together and structure it as you would a business."

KEY 4: DEFINE BUDGET AND SCHEDULE

Planning and budgeting the production phase without thinking about and planning the post–publishing phase is, unfortunately, common. You've *got* to have a plan and a budget from the moment you start thinking of publishing your manuscript. Post-publishing activities can begin *before* you write the first word of your book and no later than the moment you finish the writing process.

This is how *Wintersong* by S. Jae–Jones received an incredible amount of pre–publication buzz, resulting in over 50 thousand people shelving it as "to–read" in Goodreads. The debut author explains how she did it:

"I think buzz is a combination of luck, timing, and a commercial pitch. The luck portion is entirely out of your hands, but I do think you can affect the other two. As for timing, I don't think it hurts to start talking about your book as early as you can. I do think there can be instances of too fast, too soon, but getting the word out about your book via your social media channels (if you have them) is not a bad idea. Announce when your book goes up on Goodreads. Announce when it becomes available for preorder. Announce when you get a review. Talk about the writing or editing process. Your book needs time and exposure. There are five touch points of marketing in that a customer encounters a product five times before making a decision about whether or not to buy. The earlier you start, the more time you have for readers to encounter your work."

The longer you expose potential readers to your book, and the number of times they encounter your book, make a difference. Repetition is in the core of any advertising and marketing campaign. You can't assume that people will get your message the first time they are exposed to it. Buying a book, for the most part, isn't an impulse purchase. It's a process that might take time. Luckily, your book isn't a perishable product and the fact that you are the publisher guarantees that you won't leave it behind and move on like most publishers would when a book doesn't yield results in the first couple of months.

And when does post-publishing end? For established publishers, the answer is clear. It ends on or around the publishing date of their books. You, on the other hand, can do it whenever you want. We often go back to our small catalog and work on books that were published three years ago. Sometimes, we pivot and find new ways to reach readers and make new sales. In a digital age, your book is always new, especially if it has not yet found readers. If people loved it or thought it was worthwhile two years ago, that only reaffirms that you can find new fans now, too.

KEY 5: TREAT YOUR BOOK AS THE PRIMARY MARKETING SOURCE

Elements: Always have your book at the center of your marketing efforts and make it the primary source of your campaign. Your book already has most of the advertising and marketing elements. It should always be the first place you look for your campaign's building blocks. From log lines to posts and tweets, make use of the book's content. You can always go back to your book and find ideas that will help you create posts and messages that will keep your book alive and fresh.

Title: The title is your product's brand name. For an author, a title is an artistic choice. From a publishing perspective, choosing the right title has to be an outcome of your campaign's strategy.

Cover: The cover should be treated and structured as if it were an ad. What does this mean? The purpose of the text and the images is to *sell*. In essence, every word in the copy, the colors, the size, the fonts, the images, and the final composition count are in service of your campaign's objectives.

KEY 6: CONNECT WITH THE TRUTH

Do not over-promise. Deliver your book's most unique qualities in a measured approach. Remember that a disappointed reader can harm you with a bad review. You can't win them all, and that's fine. Taking control of your message means that you are responsible for the outcome. Always go back to the core of your book. Tell your reader exactly what they are getting.

KEY 7: OWN, CONTROL, AND MANAGE YOUR POST-PUBLISHING WORK

According to the 2018 report from ProQuest affiliate Bowker, self-publishing in the US grew at a rate of more than 28 percent in 2017, up from an 8 percent increase during the prior year. The total number of self-published titles grew from 786,935 to 1,009,188, surpassing the million mark for the first time.

These books competed with approximately 300,000 books that came out the same year by established publishers, and this number keeps growing. This is a staggering number considering that there are millions of older books from years past that are still on the market.

Why does this matter?

In a competitive and crowded marketplace, you must be ahead of the game. You do it by carving your niche—by defining and communicating your competitive edge and controlling the processes that involve branding, advertising, and marketing.

Paying other people to make decisions on your behalf without the ability to scrutinize their work is a recipe for failure. In the following chapters, we will share our analytical and practical tools to help you take control, make sound decisions, and find success.

CHAPTER 3

You are a Brand

By micropublishing your book, you have created three brand equities, all in one: a publisher, an author, and a book. Therefore, understanding how brands get developed, built, and maintained is helpful. All three brands are interconnected, and all can be dealt with separately.

If you plan to make micropublishing an ongoing effort, build your publisher brand. Any engagement with other publishers and suppliers will be easier when you approach them as an entity and not as an individual. Build a corporate identity. A name, a great logo, and you're in business.

In order to build a strong brand, you must shape how customers think and feel about it. Building your author brand will make the promotion of your next books much easier. The same goes for each unique book and your publisher brand.

Your goal is to build the right type of experiences around your brands, so that customers have specific and positive thoughts, feelings, beliefs, opinions, and perceptions about it. When you have strong brand equity, your customers will buy more from you, recommend your brands to other people, and hopefully become part of your growing fanbase. These are the steps you need to take:

STEP 1: BRAND IDENTITY—WHO ARE YOU?

Your goal is to create brand awareness. You need to make sure that your brand stands out, and that customers recognize it. You're also trying to ensure that brand perceptions are *correct*. In order for your brand to be correct, you have to know who you are. Who are you as a publisher? An author? What is your Book ID? When you know the answers to these questions, you'll be able to communicate them to others.

STEP 2: BRAND MEANING—WHAT ARE YOU?

When you look at your book from a branding perspective, you have to conceptualize your reader's reading experience and how well your book meets your readers' needs and satisfies their expectations on a deeper level, emotional or psychological.

STEP 3: BRAND RESPONSE—WHAT DO I THINK, OR FEEL, ABOUT YOU?

Your readers' responses to your book fall into two categories: judgments and feelings. Judgment is when the readers judge your book on its overall merits. But also, whether the things that are said about the book answered the reader's expectation. Feelings relates to how they feel about your book.

STEP 4: BRAND RESONANCE. HOW MUCH OF A CONNECTION WOULD I LIKE TO HAVE WITH YOU?

You have achieved brand resonance when your readers feel a bond with your brand. This is what you'll achieve:

1. Behavioral loyalty: Your readers love your book, and they see it as a special purchase and would most likely read other books of yours.
2. Sense of community: Your readers feel a sense of community with other people who feel strongly about

you or your book and consider themselves your readers, or your fans.

3. Active engagement: This is the strongest example of brand loyalty. Readers are actively engaged with you and your books. This could include joining a fan club, following you on social media, participating in online chats, readings, signings, and other events.

CHAPTER 4

From Who You Are to a Fully-Fledged Campaign

Now you have arrived at the stage where your real work on your book's post-publishing campaign begins. From figuring out the market to composing effective ads. From understanding how every word you say about your book can make a difference and how to target your readers.

Let's start by defining "who are you" and "what are you" in as many details as possible. Begin by gathering data about the market, the competition, and your potential readers. These are the things you should look at:

- The success of books similar to yours on the Amazon Best Seller rank.
- Their author's ranking.
- The amount of reviews these books garnered.
- How many years they've been in the market.
- Their marketing strategy and how it was implemented.
- Book titles, cover designs, and cover texts.
- Other books' product pages.
- Authors' websites and social media presences. Read interviews with the authors.

Is there an interest in your book's subject matter? Many great products have created markets and invoked "hidden" interest. Most tap into an existing interest. Here you have to determine how your book can garner interest in an existing market with similar books. If your book has to compete in a saturated market, your goal will be to separate it from the rest of the pack.

Where is the market for your book? Is it local? Is it global? Is it the size of an area code? Or is it in another country/language?

Who are your competitors?

a. Are they books?
b. Are they authors?
c. Are they publishers?
d. What makes them competitors?
e. What are their strengths and weaknesses?

Based on the above, what is your advantage? An advantage can be derived from the book's theme, market conditions, timing, events that can give you leverage, an exposure opportunity, or a sudden interest that should prompt action on your end.

What is the USP and MUQ? What make your books stand out?

Who are our customers? An accurate targeted profile of your customers comprised of age, gender, interests, and many more variables.

What is the point of entry? Is there a period of the year, an event, or circumstances that help the launch of the book?

What is the cost? How much would it cost to create an effective campaign and what is your projected return on investment. If you can't answer these questions now, you should determine how much money you can/intend to spend on the campaign. You have to budget at least 3 months from the date of publication.

What would be a desirable outcome of your campaign? You can answer this with the number of copies sold, money earned, or any other objective you set up. As we discussed before, a desirable outcome doesn't have to be making your investment back. It could be a long–term investment to launch your writing career, which would yield income later on.

Based on all the information and answers you've gathered, you'll move to the next phase in which you will:

Configure your Book ID and Book Passport: Create an accurate advertising and marketing profile of your book and define the strategy for your campaign.

Configure your Reader ID: Create an accurate profile of your readers.

Configure your Author ID: Create a profile of your author brand.

Configure a campaign: Create the actual elements of your campaign: ads, posts, pictures, and videos.

Reach readers: Put your campaign to work. Use free and paid media platforms. Drive traffic to your website and product page, and create awareness and demand. Build a mailing list of potential readers.

Make a sale: Bring potential readers to take action and buy your book.

Go Global: Reach readers in other countries. Sell translation rights for your book in other countries in as many languages as you can.

Manage your readers: Build ongoing relationships with your readers and make them want your next book. Expand your author brand and reach more readers.

CHAPTER 5

Configure Your Book ID

The Book ID will help you define and create your advertising and marketing strategy. It's a proven tool that evolves over time and will accompany you in all aspects of publishing and post–publishing.

A Book ID comprises the following elements:

- The book's profile.
- The book's unique qualities.
- The book's unique selling points.
- Target audience: readers and customers.
- Market: leaders, competition, and geography.
- The message.

Configure your Book ID by filling in a worksheet with information and answers. Some are straightforward questions, and some are analytical.

WHAT IS YOUR BOOK PROFILE?

Define the following:

a. Genre: Fiction or Nonfiction.
b. Category and subcategory.

c. Theme and style—additional valuable information that is unique to your book.

Example: This is how we configured *The Flea*'s profile:

Genre and category: Nonfiction, Sports Biography, Sports, Soccer, Children's soccer book, Children's sports book. These would also serve as the main search words.

Theme: Coming of age of the world's greatest soccer star.

Style: Nonfiction written as fiction.

CONFIGURE THE MUQ

What is the Most Unique Quality of the book?

Example: *The Flea*'s Most Unique Quality is its storytelling style, namely, a biography that reads like a novel. The MUQ can also be the book's USP. The MUQ is a quality integrated with and internal to the book, unlike an external USP, such as the price of the book.

How do you identify your book's MUQ?

It could be your writing style. It could be your hero. It could be a new approach to the subject matter. It could be a combination of genres.

CONFIGURE THE USP

The Unique Sale Point bridges between your book and the reader. It is a quality in your book that differentiates it from its competitors and is often the book's MUQ. Think of it as what your book has that similar books don't. Defining the USP is the first step, followed by communicating it to your readers. You should articulate the USP so it will stand out. A USP is the pillar of your message. For example, although our MUQ is, "A biography that is read like a novel," our USP could be, "The coming–of–age story of Leo Messi," or "The #1 Leo Messi international bestseller," or, "The critically acclaimed book loved by parents and kids alike." All three have one or two elements that are unique to our book. These are translated into messages, slogans, headers, texts, and so on, making a case for why to choose our offering over the competition.

TARGET AUDIENCE

Readers and customers: Targeting is about interest, demographics, gender, age groups, behavior, purchase habits, locals, languages, and a few more characteristics such as marital status, profession, and more. Targeting is the most critical phase of any campaign after you have correctly defined the USP and MUQ. Oftentimes, these go hand in hand. An accurate profile of your customer is the cornerstone of any successful campaign.

It's often confusing to define whom your readers are and whom your customers are. In our case, the specific reader demographic is between ages 9–14, but this isn't necessarily our customer's demographic. Parents and grandparents are more inclined to buy a book for their kids.

MARKET: LEADERS, COMPETITORS, AND GEOGRAPHY

Defining your market is essential because your targeting will be much more accurate, and thus more effective. Defining the market is related to your book profile, competitors, and geography. This is where you distinguish your book from other books in your market with a variety of reasons. They have the same theme or subject matter, they are in similar categories, or they aim for the same reader's profile and demographic. Those who are already published and the ones that will join the competition later. Identify your market leaders and analyze how you can stand out and become a leader.

This is how we assessed the market. There were adult biographies on Messi but almost none for children, and none that focused on his coming-of-age story. We learned our market and we understood the competition. We knew that we had a distinct product and were therefore able to position it in the right way. That is how we carved a niche in the market.

THE MESSAGE

The message is the product of your Book ID components. Start with creating a master message. An effective message contains a mixture of emotional and substantive components. Emotional components make the connection and substantive components supply the reasoning. We'll elaborate later.

CHAPTER 6

Message Formats

Your objectives will determine what platforms, means, and formats are best for you. Platforms are social networks, email messaging services, websites, blogs, product pages, landing pages, printed ads, and your book. Formats are the actual content such as posts, blogs, emails, ads, and stories. Means are text, voice, still images, and videos.

Here are examples of three message formats that are commonly used:

A PITCH

What it is: A description that conveys the book's main elements.

Objective: Inform and attract interest.

Elements: Story, MUQ, USP.

Platforms: Use it as a back cover or book page synopsis, in email messaging and landing pages.

Media: All.

Means: All.

Length: 30–80 words.

Example: "*The Flea* is the captivating story of soccer legend Lionel Messi, from his first touch at age five in the streets of Rosario, Argentina, to his first goal on the Camp Nou pitch in

Barcelona, Spain. *The Flea* tells the amazing story of a boy who overcame growth deficiency to play the beautiful game and was destined to become the world's greatest soccer player. Michael Part is the bestselling author of *Cristiano Ronaldo—The Rise of a Winner*. His books are sold in 36 countries and loved by children and parents alike.

A HOOK

What it is: A short sentence/slogan that encapsulates the essence of your message and makes it stand out.

Objective: Attract and draw attention.

Elements: MUQ, USP.

Platforms: Use it in ads, landing pages, and short posts. It can be used as a header, text, and slogan.

Media: All.

Means: All.

Length: 1–15 words.

Examples:

- "One Million copies sold!"
- "From the slums of Rio to the world's top!"
- "Every kid who dreams of playing with the German National Team should read this book!"

The main element in these three hooks is *success*. In the first, it's the success of the book. In the second, it's the success of the hero. In the third, it alludes to the potential success of the reader. The second also summarizes the storyline—from rags to riches. The third also speaks to a specific target audience and geography.

LOGLINE

What it is: A short sentence summarizing the main storyline. This can be used as a header or main text of a post or an ad. The logline is a bit more elaborate than the hook, and more focused on the USP of the book.

Objective: Attract and draw attention.

Elements: USP.

Media: All.

Means: All.

Length: 10–20 words.

Example: "The kid who was told he would never grow up, and grew up to become the world's best soccer player!"

CTA: CALL TO ACTION

What it is: An effective message should have a soft or hard call to action such as, "Learn More," or, "Buy Now," and when elaborated upon, could serve as the main message.

Objective: Create a sense of urgency and encourage the recipient to take action.

Elements: USP.

Media: All.

Means: All.

Length: 2–12 words

Example: Get your free copy today!

MHI: MUST HAVE INFORMATION

This is the basic information that has to be included in your message. We'll talk about it later when we discuss how to compose an effective message.

Once you've configured your Book ID, start with composing texts into the three aforementioned formats. Later, we'll analyze how each word plays a role in the message. At this stage, you have to craft the building blocks of your message. You can write a few different texts in each format and post them. This will give you an idea of how effective your message is. What works and what doesn't. And at times, it will demand challenging your Book ID configuration.

CHAPTER 7

Configure Your Book Passport

The **Book Passport** elements to configure:
1. The book's success.
2. The author's recognition.
3. The universal and global appeal of the book.

THE BOOK'S SUCCESS

This refers to a book that has already been published, as well as a new book that is part of a series. Objective measures of your book's success rate include:

- **Sales!** Any significant number you can provide (as low as 10,000) would be the first thing any publisher or editor would look at.
- **Translation rights sold:** If you've already made translation rights deals, you should mention in what language(s), and who the foreign publisher(s) who bought the rights is/are. This is not only useful information, it also draws publishers' attention.
- **Ranking:** Your book's listing on Amazon and other bestseller lists is helpful. A favorable sales ranking in a specific category may be good enough.

- **Longevity:** How many days, weeks, months, or even years your book or series of books has been actively sold.
- **Reviews:** The grade and amount of positive reviews the book garnered.

What may come as a surprise to you is that you can still do without a significant achievement in any of the above.

THE AUTHOR'S RECOGNITION

This is comprised of the author's body of work, bestseller listings, reviews, and public name recognition. This could also be relevant to new authors who are about to publish their first book or have just recently published their first book, if they gained professional and/or public standing before they wrote the book.

UNIVERSAL AND GLOBAL APPEAL

Does your book have elements that are universal, and can it appeal to people everywhere, or in a certain country or countries? In the case of *The Flea*, the worldwide interest in soccer star Lionel Messi and the "rags–to–riches" story at the heart of Messi's rise to stardom enhanced the book's global appeal.

CHAPTER 8

Go Global:
Sell Your Translated Book
in Dozens of Countries.

Had we not opened to the possibility of reaching out to the world, we wouldn't have gotten very far. Working toward global reach enabled us not only to sell many more books, but gave us the flexibility to find success in other markets if things didn't go our way in the US. Within the world markets, a book could perform in one or two or even forty markets, so the performance in the US is only one part of a much larger picture.

So, by definition, whether you consider yourself a self–published author or a micropublisher, opening your offerings to the world will multiply the chances that your books will be exposed and sold to more readers. When you look beyond your own language and market, you might strike gold.

The following keys explain the benefits of going global and provide a very detailed roadmap to achieving a translation rights deal.

KEY #1: OPEN TO THE WORLD AND GET REWARDED!

If you own your books' translation rights, you are good to go. And why not? You've already done most of the work. Going global could be a great part of your journey and, frankly, overlooking the enormous potential of going global doesn't make much sense.

KEY #2: TECHNOLOGY MAKES PUBLISHING YOUR BOOK GLOBALLY SO MUCH EASIER AND YOU SHOULD TAP INTO IT!

Most SPs, micropublishers, and even midsized publishers aren't into global publishing. Why? You can list half a dozen reasons why, "It's not for me." Let's have a look at just a few, and we'll try to tackle them:

My book didn't sell well in the US, so what are my chances in selling it elsewhere in the world? Many books can still be sold globally without a local track record.

My book has nothing in it that can attract a foreign publisher, or a foreign reader. Look again! Most books have a universal MUQ or a universal appeal, and some have appeal in certain countries.

Micropublishing was hard. Going global seems much harder. Actually, you've done most of the hard work already. You have a book and you've already taken many crucial steps. Going global demands more work, but it isn't as hard as you might suspect.

Micropublishing was a costly process. Going global could be a tall order, time–consuming, and costly. Going global could involve no risks and you could get paid in advance.

Our advice: Don't give up just yet!

KEY #3: THINGS YOU MUST KNOW ABOUT GLOBAL PUBLISHING BEFORE YOU "PACK" YOUR BOOK FOR THE JOURNEY:

A **translation rights deal** is when you license your book's rights to a foreign publisher.

What are you licensing? The rights to translate, publish, and sell your books in a certain language in a certain territory (or worldwide) for a certain period.

What to do? You should negotiate a deal with a local publisher and sign a contract. You can do it directly or with an agent. When you do it with local professionals, the entire publishing process is the responsibility of the publisher, and the publisher incurs 100% on their expense, which mostly has benefits (just a few drawbacks). As we'll explain later, if you get a deal from a foreign publisher, your chances of success are much higher.

KEY #4: YOU SHOULD OWN TERRITORIAL AND TRANSLATION RIGHTS OF YOUR BOOK

Book rights are sold in different geographical areas of the world and in different languages. The term most commonly used is "Territorial Rights," which are split into three categories.

1. North American English, which includes the US and Canada.
2. English language rights in the remainder of the world, which includes the UK, Commonwealth countries or former Commonwealth Countries (Australia, New Zealand, South Africa, etc., excluding Canada).
3. Translation rights. The rights for the non–English speaking world. These rights can be sold to a country or countries where a certain official language is dominant. For example, the rights to Spanish can be sold to a specific country or multiple territories where Spanish is the official language as well as to all of Latin America

and Spain. In addition, the rights can be granted to a language for sale in the entire world.

As the author and publisher of your books, we assume that you own all the rights. Most authors who license the rights to an American publisher own all other territorial and translation rights. Hence, the first thing you should do is check if you have control of the rights, and what rights you own. It is always helpful to make sure that your rights are secured and copyrighted with the Library of Congress.

The scope of translation rights: The territorial and translation rights that you own enable you to license your books to other publishers in the world, and, of course, to publish them yourself. The term "licensing" is used because you are not selling the rights outright. You license the use of the intellectual property you own, for a certain language, to a certain territory(s), and for a restricted period of time. When the licensing period expires, those rights revert to you.

Most translation rights deals are made for a period of 5–7 years. We'll get to specifics later when we'll analyze in detail the translation rights agreement.

KEY #5: LICENSING TRANSLATION RIGHTS OR MICROPUBLISHING IN A FOREIGN LANGUAGE

Licensing: The key players involved in the sale of translation rights could be literary agents, scouts, or editors whose job is to buy translation rights.

When you have an offer from a publisher, you must negotiate a deal with the local publisher and sign a contract. You can do it directly with the publisher or through an agent.

The benefits are:

- The entire publishing process is the responsibility of the publisher, and the publisher incurs 100% on their expense.

- In most cases, you get an advance that is deducted from future sales. Later, if your book sells, you'll earn royalties computed as a percentage of the retail price of each copy.
- By the end of the term, the rights revert to you or go up for renewal.

The downsides:

- You don't have control of the publishing process.
- Publishers commit to publishing your book within a period of 18 months. So, if you want your book to be published sooner, you might be disappointed.
- The royalty payments could stretch into 6 months of the following year after the book was published, so it may take a long time until you get your first royalties.

Micropublishing: The process of publishing in a foreign language is similar to the work you did in your own market. You ran the show yourself from start to finish. Translation, followed by the entire production process: proof, cover design, layout, promotion, as well as printing (if you publish a printed book), distribution, and sales.

The benefits are:

- You control the entire process.
- The release date is under your control.
- You get compensated much faster and you get 30–60% of the sale price versus 6–10% in a licensing deal.

The downsides are:

- You operate in a totally unknown marketplace.
- Your distribution channels are limited.
- You have to communicate with your readers in a foreign language.

CHAPTER 9

Pitching Your Book to Foreign Publishers and Agents

There are two approaches you should consider. One is the blanket approach and the other is the targeted approach. The blanket approach is to reach as many publishers and foreign agents in as many countries as possible. The targeted approach is to filter the publishers and foreign agents who would be more likely to respond. These are the pros and cons for both approaches:

THE BLANKET APPROACH

1. You never know who might respond, and if you are new to this process, the blanket approach could be a first step in establishing yourself as a publisher and author. You could look at it as an effort to say to the world, "Here I am." It's a statement you make about yourself and about the fact that you think your book could be successful in foreign markets. Yet, you should be aware that coming out of virtually nowhere and presenting your case means that you should be very concise and

thoughtful in the way you communicate, which means: don't overpromise, don't oversell. Try to pitch your book accurately and subtly while delivering your message effectively.

2. Email correspondences with publishers and agents is common practice in the industry, and if you have a valuable message, it won't be treated as spam.

3. It's easier to work with big lists where you don't put a lot of effort in filtering the list because the recipient does that for you. In many cases, based on a targeted subject line, the recipients may or may not open your email. But they may glance at your name and the book's name, and this connection might prove useful in future engagements.

THE TARGETED APPROACH

Filtering and targeting requires a lot of work, time, and attention, but could yield much better results. You can do it manually by gathering information from publishers' websites.

This is what you have to do if you would like to do it yourself:

1. Eliminate publishers who do not buy translation rights.

2. The next cut would be between nonfiction and fiction publishers. Publishers who do only nonfiction won't respond to your fiction book. If they don't do nonfiction, why bother them with your nonfiction book?

3. From here, you zoom in to publishers who have published books that are within your book's category, genre, and target audience. The more specific you go, the more accurately you can hit your target. For example, if your book's subject is medical problems during pregnancy, you should target publishers who publish popular medical books, and for those who already have books about pregnancy, your book could complement their list.

4. Look out for publishers who have bought translation rights for books that have similarities to your book. This is a telling sign that the publisher might be interested in your book, because they responded to the book's group, category, genre, and demographic. If you sell children's books, you should communicate with publishers who buy rights for this demographic, and the more specific you are—specifying age, subjects, even book style and themes—the better response you are likely to get.

5. Finally, look to publishers in countries that may respond favorably to elements in your book. If your cookbook is about Middle Eastern cooking, you might find a great market in Western and Northern Europe, where there is great interest in this cuisine.

HOW TO COMMUNICATE WITH FOREIGN PUBLISHERS

This is how you should grab the foreign editor/publisher's attention—through your message structure, content, and design. There are three layers to an effective message:

1. The must have information.
2. Text based on the USP (Unique Sale Point) of your book.
3. Call to action.

MUST HAVE INFORMATION

1. The title, author's name, and publisher's name.
2. Synopsis of the book, author's resume, and publisher's resume.
3. Categories, genre, and demographic.
4. ISBN.
5. Translation rights information, i.e., what languages you have already sold the book in, along with the name of the local publisher.

6. Your contact information.
7. Links to reviews and your social media pages.
8. Front cover image, and a photograph of the author.

CREATE AN EFFECTIVE MESSAGE

This is always the most challenging part. Use your Book Passport and Book ID—they should be very helpful in this process. Here are a few essential points to make your work much easier:

Goal/objective: Define what you want to accomplish and know your limitations. You have a few seconds to grab the recipient's attention. Giving information isn't enough. You should grab attention, and our approach is that when you contact a foreign publisher, although your ultimate goal is, of course, to make a sale, the first and most important goal is to invoke **interest**. You should focus on exactly that. That is precisely why the email subject line is crucial.

Subject line: Write a short engaging sentence that will draw the recipient's attention and make him open your mail. Don't sell. Don't overpromise. Try to project into the subject line a sense of objective perspective and, at the same time, instill a hook that will pull the levers of your target audience.

USP: When we first sent out a message about *The Flea*, our USP was Leo Messi. A secondary but important sales point was the fact that the author—although it was his first book—was a successful Disney screenwriter. These were the two main sales points we worked with. So even if this is your first foray in the foreign market and you can't rely on sales or recognition, you might find your USP in the universal and global appeal of the book. You could use association to other successful books that are similar, or anything in the content of the book that could be attractive to single or multiple markets. For example, a book about a Brazilian boy who saves a penguin who has gotten stuck in an oil slick. First, you should look for publishers who have an environmental category. It could also be interesting to Brazilian publishers. In some countries like Germany, children's books about penguins have been successful, so you might get some response there. This is a real example of how we create shortlists of publishers that might show interest. At times, you should use different USPs for different countries.

Copy: You are not a professional copywriter, but you are a writer. You could learn pretty quickly how to compose an effective message. *Remember: This is not a query letter. This is an ad.*

Structure: You are creating an ad that has two headlines, one in the subject line and one at the top of your email. Then comes a subheader, followed by the body of text which includes the synopsis, the author's bio, and, at the bottom, the MHI.

Content: Attract attention. Communicate the USP and call to action. The copy should be informative and must contain the reasoning every publisher in the world wants to know: Why your book would be a great investment for them.

Image: Use your front cover picture along with any other picture that supports your message, such as your other books in a series or an image that has relevance to the book and reflects the USP.

CHAPTER 10

How to Build Your Author Brand

Whether you just published your first book, or you have been doing it for a while, branding yourself is a crucial step in reaching readers and building your readership base for years to come.

Looking at yourself as a brand might seem strange to you, but from a marketing point of view, it's as important as treating your book as a product. You should detach yourself from your book in order to do an effective job as a publisher—the same thinking applies here. Separation from your "author self" is essential to your success.

Author brand is critical for building a body of work, and it will prove its worth when you write more than one book. During this process, your author brand will be a more powerful marketing tool than your individual books.

You probably don't know each of John Grisham's books by their titles, but his name stands out for bestselling, well-crafted mysteries and legal thrillers. Grisham as a brand is much more famous than any book he wrote. Deepak Chopra is a brand name for New Age books. Do you remember all his book titles? Probably not. Philip Roth is a brand name associated with modern classic American novels, and most of us would find it hard to name all of his books.

From a marketing standpoint, the author is more brandable than their books—although some book series, or their protagonists, are very successful brands in themselves.

The challenge is, what do you do when you are still unknown, and your book barely sells? How should you prioritize your efforts? The answer is, you should intertwine your individual book and your author brand into one coherent message.

Let us walk you through the process of putting together the foundation for your author brand.

AWARENESS, ACCEPTANCE, AND SEPARATION

The change begins with your awareness and acceptance. Awareness that detaching your public author identity from your real self is something you ought to do, and acceptance that you should switch your mindset from thinking and acting like an author to thinking and acting like a publisher.

The first step is configuring your Author ID separately from the Book ID. But in order to be successful in this process, you should consider creating an Author ID that consists of an author persona that doesn't necessarily mirror yourself or your writing. It's a unique and separate professional persona. It's not about creating a fake entity—it's about what you'd like to expose to the world and use publicly. It's the attire you wear for work—not what you wear at home. **The author brand is a constant**. Building your brand makes sense because you are the constant and your brand can be nurtured to grow over time.

CONFIGURING YOUR AUTHOR ID

There are three main phases in the evolution of your author brand.

1. The unknown.

2. The read and unknown.
3. The read and known: the branded author.

The Unknown: How does an unknown author become a brand? Your first efforts should be quite simple and straightforward. As a first-time author with no public or professional background to show, you should start with those who already know you. Use social media in the early stages of your writing process to spread the word. Create an author page on Facebook, Instagram, Twitter, and Goodreads. Invite your friends to join. Most of them would be thrilled to know that you authored a book. Although you are focused on writing, bring your close circles to the process early on. Let them know. Share your experience.

But more importantly, be serious about what you do. Introduce yourself as an author. Do not just portray a picture of yourself as someone who happens to write a book. Like many first timers, you might have a day job, and even if your close circle of family friends and colleagues are in the know, they will not treat you as a professional if you won't insist on it. The public perception will change only if you treat yourself as a pro and communicate this to others. More about creating an effective social media presence later.

You should make a list of potential readers and potential social communicators. Friends, family, and acquaintances that will help you create and promote your new venture as an author. Your message is as important as (and maybe more important than) the platform. Take a look at these two examples. The difference in the approach and positioning is crucial, although the content is almost the same.

A text about a book party, which reads:

"Author Veronica Smith will be our guest, reading from her critically-acclaimed new book…" versus:

"We are throwing a party for our friend, Veronica, who wrote a great book about…"

The first post positions Veronica Smith as a critically-acclaimed author. The second as a friend of the host who happened to write a book, and whose last name no one will remember because it wasn't mentioned…

You should work hard to make this distinction, and this will be your first step in becoming known as an author, not as a friend on Facebook.

The Read and Unknown: This is the phase in which you've already published a book or two, and you might have a fairly sizable number of readers, but you're not big enough to have name recognition. You should work on creating the link between your books and the author. When people mention your work, your status should be changed from, "The book about…" to, "A book by…"

Obviously, this is a challenging thing to do. If you are a one-off writer, it might not be as important for you. But if you intend to write more books, and as you garner readership, you should help your readers make the connection between the book they read and the books they haven't yet read by the common denominator: You.

What to do: Focus your efforts in building your author brand by letting people know that you are a published author and that you are worth their attention. It might sound strange, but you should at times be more focused on the number of people who know your name than the number of people who read your books.

Relevance: Identify the relevance of your book to current events or a topic that has public interest at the time of release. Contact news outlets and let them know about your book and its relevancy to the news, so they might invite you to their show as an expert. With a fiction book, you might find an angle that can appeal to audiences' interests and, in both instances, look for the topic/angle/thread in your book that can be interesting to a large audience, and own the subject you are talking about.

Learn how to deliver it in an effective way verbally and in all written forms.

The Read and Known—the Branded Author: Getting to this stage means that you have built a body of work and that you have garnered a readership that has read your books and is keen to read more books by you, and that your name as an author is defined not only by your books, but by your public presence and stature. At this stage, your main goal is to do what you probably like best: write.

CHAPTER 11

How to Get Your Message Across

As social media platforms limit your organic exposure in order to make you pay for advertising, it becomes difficult to gain free-of-charge visibility. Still, it is worthwhile exploring the free-of-charge options that could work perfectly fine and yield great results. Emailing is the most cost-effective way to communicate with your readers or publishers around the world. The effort you put into building your email list is one of the best investments you can make. Having access to the inboxes of your future readers means that you can continue to build and nurture relationships over time. Then, when it's time for your next book, you'll be communicating directly with the readers or editors that already know you and will in turn help grow your readership and your author brand. Your email list is yours, free and clear. Start building the list by accumulating contacts from your personal lists, and fans and friends from your blog, website, and social media accounts. Encourage them to sign up for your email list. Create a sign-up form and offer something in exchange. The first thing that comes to mind is likely your book, but that's not necessarily all you have to offer.

Use an email service provider (ESP). The ESP will provide you with all the tools, templates, and services you need to get subscribers, test your campaigns, and manage the day-to-day requirements of your list. There are free services you can choose from with which you can reach thousands of readers without spending a dime, and the paid services give you more features and aren't expensive.

Guest blogging is a great strategy for getting high-quality inbound links to your site, increasing your visibility, and of course getting new subscribers for your list. You can offer other writers to be your guests and a plug on your list in exchange for a plug on theirs.

A properly executed guest blogging strategy can yield a strong ROI, and supports your SEO, social media, and email marketing efforts simultaneously.

It makes sense: the people who visit your blog post or webpage are looking for something specific, so your CTA needs to meet those unique needs. For instance, if you've got a ton of traffic visiting your "writing tips" blog article, why not entice those people to subscribe to your email list by including a simple CTA like this: "Click here to download a free writing tip."

Your *About Us* page is one of the most potent pages in terms of conversion potential. Think about it—how often do you visit *About Us* pages for businesses you don't care about?

But even if you don't have a blog or website, and your social media presence is small, start building your email list with your family and friends. Approach your close contacts first and ask them for emails of five friends who might be interested in your book. Then create a link to the book file, a PDF, Kindle, or ePub version, and email or send a text message to your contacts about it. Once you have several hundred contacts, you can ask your readers to post reviews or recommend the book to their friends.

Ultimately, if you want to break out and reach a wider audience, you'll have to use paid advertising. We found Facebook (and Instagram) to be the best platforms for our books. You should also consider Amazon and other platforms like Bookbub and Goodreads.

In the next few chapters, will show you how to create effective ads and email/text messages based on your book ID. It works for us time and again, and it should work for you too.

CHAPTER 12

How to Create an Effective Ad

Maintaining an active presence on social media is the name of the game. The challenging part is how to implement the building blocks of your Book ID into great posts and effective ads.

Here is how you do it: assemble all the elements of your Book ID, and study them. Then answer the following questions:

1. What is the USP and MUQ of the book?
2. What is the target audience of the book (readers and customers)?
3. What is the geography?
4. Where is the market?
5. What do I want to achieve?
6. What is the message?
7. What is the message format?

THE MAIN COPY ELEMENTS

Once you answer these questions, it's time to compose your messages on Facebook, Amazon, Google, and so on. No matter which platform you choose, most ads and posts consistently incorporate certain elements that are the carriers of your message.

1. Connect: Use the third person to communicate with the reader.
2. Title: The name of the book.
3. Emotion: Use words that create an emotional impact.
4. Objective Authority: Use a quote from a known name.
5. Superlative: Use favorable words to portray your book.
6. Theme: Describe the genre and style of your book.
7. Reader: Describe the reader your book is aimed at.
8. Author: The author's brand name.
9. Success: The success of the book or of related books.
10. Association: Use a known name of an author or a book to reflect on your book.
11. Promise: The benefits of the book for your reader. From emotional experience to valuable information.
12. Facts: Use facts to support your argument.
13. Call to Action: Everything you do has to culminate in what you want the ad reader to do. From "Learn more," to "Buy now."
14. MHI: Must have information

AD PROTOTYPES

There are several used ad prototypes, and multiple prototypes that combine the following four elements. When you compose an ad, be aware that every word has meaning, so you should be very precise with your word choices.

Association ads connect your book with a reference to other books or authors that the reader might know about, and they make a shortcut because they assume that the reader would draw from the comparison.

A subcategory of the association ad is the **success ad**, in which you associate your work with the success of other books/ authors, or even that of your other books.

A **quote ad** is one in which the main text is a quote from a review by a reader, an author, or a critic.

A **story ad** should reflect the essence of the book using its storytelling style, and can be useful in the early stages of your campaign. You don't have reviews or anything to show for it but the book, and that's okay. When done right, it could work very well.

A **promise ad** is one that focuses on the reading experience or the benefits the readers will get. It uses emotional terms and emphasizes the reader's need. It might offer a solution to a problem, and usually connects directly with the reader.

HOW TO COMPOSE YOUR ADS

Even for a skilled writer, transforming into a copywriter could prove tricky. Copywriting is an acquired writing method that can be learned and practiced. The text has to create an impact with a limited amount of words. You answer the seven questions we introduced in the beginning of the chapter, and you choose an ad prototype and what kind of message you'd like to incorporate.

Now you should transform the common elements into words and compose a concise sentence. You should remember that each word is a building block in the sentence that could fulfill multiple tasks.

A great way to learn how it should be done is by analyzing other people's ads. You could learn from the good *and* the bad while perfecting your copywriting skills. It takes a lot of trial and error, but there is a point at which you should know exactly how to compose a successful ad.

Here are examples that analyze multiple ads. You can see how common elements transform into words and sentences, and are linked to the Book ID, target audiences, etc., but most of all, address the goal/objective of your campaign. Each word plays a role or multiple roles in the text, and the entire composition sums up into an effective text.

ASSOCIATION AD

The association ad brings up other successful books, and intends to provoke an immediate emotional response and sell the book's theme right away. When using a reference, you should have your target audience in mind. If they are young, the reference should be more contemporary.

ASSOCIATION AD: LOGLINE

The following association ad invokes a classic film. It would work for a certain age group of people who know the reference.

Example: *"If you liked Silence of the Lambs, you'll love Dead End Girl."*

Let's break down the text. Each word plays a part in building the overall impact:

"If you"—Element: connection.

"Liked"—Elements: emotion and promise.

"If you liked"—In three words, the text combines three elements. It's a great example of how to create a concise and dynamic copy that very economically communicates your message to the recipient.

"Silence of the Lambs"—Element: association. This is the reference that aims to create the desired impact. It creates an association with success, and also connects to the genre.

"You'll love Dead End Girl"—Elements: connection, emotion (love), and introduction of the title, *Dead End Girl* (which is also a MHI).

With only 12 words, the writer of this ad created a multilayered text using six elements. The text makes a connection with the recipient in invoking their memories, likes, and urges. There is a "hidden CTA" because it drives the reader to get the book without explicitly urging them to do so.

ASSOCIATION AD: HOOK

The following association ad brings up the best known and most successful names in the genre. It works on two levels. It defines the genre and strikes a chord with their readers. The second half of the text focuses on the author—the subject of the ad—who compares himself to the big names that were mentioned previously, using two pieces of supporting evidence to buttress his comparison: *The Wall Street Journal*, which he uses as an objective authority, and the number of copies of his book sold, which validates the comparison and sheds light on his amazing achievement. This is a great way to build an author brand. It makes a connection between a relatively unknown author and the genre's most successful authors while forming a solid argument. The text combines emotional and factual elements in just 18 words.

Example: *"Love Grisham, Connelly, or Child? Try Scott Pratt, the Wall Street Journal and two million-copy bestselling author."*

Elements breakdown:

"Love"—Elements: connection and emotion.

"Grisham, Connelly, or Child"—Elements: association and success

"Try Scott Pratt"—Element: author.

"The Wall Street Journal"—Elements: objective authority.

"Two million-copy bestselling author"—Elements: success, superlatives, and facts.

QUOTE AD

A positive quote from a review, or a fellow author blurb, is essential to bringing attention to your book. The number of good reviews from readers translates to your search engine position and is more valued than the few professional critics' reviews. We'll discuss later how to receive and accumulate real, genuine reviews and leverage the good ones into great ads. But at the very beginning, when you don't have reviews, a quote will do. Any media mention can be used as a quote, as we'll show later. A quote ad should contain the best and most concise words that have to answer to your ad objective. The following is a basic quote ad that gives the reader all they need to know in just nine words.

QUOTE AD: LOGLINE

A straightforward text that delivers the basics elements to the reader.

Example: *"The Wolfe is a brilliant comedic thriller"—The Irish Post.*

Elements breakdown:

"The Wolfe"—Element: title.

"Brilliant"—Element: superlative.

"Comedic"—Element: genre.

"Thriller"—Element: genre.

"The Irish Post"—Element: objective authority.

QUOTE AD: HOOK

A hook is a more complex and layered, yet still short, message that has an array of elements to attract the reader. With only 11 words, the following ad succeeds in working on multiple levels.

Example: *"The End of the Day—Engaging, charming debut thriller."—Publishers Weekly*

Elements breakdown:

"The End of the Day"—Element: title.

"*Engaging, charming*"—Element: superlatives, promise, emotion.

"*Debut*"—Elements: a fact, emotion (a sense of discovery).

"*Thriller*"—Elements: genre, emotion.

"*Publishers Weekly*"—Objective authority.

The first two words, engaging and charming, are not the usual words used to describe a thriller, and they elevate the book by emphasizing unique qualities that combine romance novel wording and that of a thriller.

The quote is taken out of a larger text, and it seems that the advertiser had a certain target audience in mind. At the same time, these three words—"engaging," "charming," and "thriller"—carry an emotional impact and a promise. This is a great way to create a very economical, multilayered text.

A STORY AD

Conveying the essence of your book, or its spirit, isn't a simple task. Doing it with very little words could be even tougher. The following examples show how you can say many things about your book using its story and style elements in the text. It's similar to a movie ad, in which a few shots work on multiple levels.

A STORY AD: HOOK

This ad delivers a storyline, the style, and the genre in just four words. In the next six, it connects with the reader emotionally, and amplifies the impact in a surprising way.

Example: "*Two days. Fourteen dead. The next victim could be you.*"

Elements breakdown:

"*Two days. Fourteen dead*"—Elements: genre, style.

"The next victim could be you"—Elements: emotion, connection.

STORY AD: PITCH

This ad creates engagement based on the book's narrative. The CTA incorporates a sense of urgency.

Example: *"Will Zombie and his friends survive? Get your copy today and find out."*

Elements breakdown:

"Will Zombie and his friends Survive"—Elements: genre, connection, and emotion.

"Get your copy today and find out"—Elements: CTA, connection, emotion.

A PROMISE AD: PITCH

The following is a great example of pitching the subject matter of the book by placing the reader's need in the center, written in an engaging style that wants you to know more.

Example: *"Picture your children saying, 'I can handle that!' after reading this book and learning that they are capable of handling their own everyday problems!"*

Elements breakdown:

"Picture"—Element: connection.

"Your children"—Elements: emotion, reader.

"After reading this book and learning"—Element: promise.

A PROMISE AD: HOOK

This ad sets up a problem and promises a solution. It's a common text for *How-To* guides and *Self-Help* books.

Example: *"Feeling stuck, lost, or unmotivated about your career and life? Learn the leadership hack that gets your drive, focus, and motivation going again."*

Elements breakdown:

"Feeling stuck...life?"—Elements: connection, reader, emotion.

"Learn the leadership hack...again"—Elements: promise, CTA.

COMBINATION ADS

Mixing ad prototypes is common. Here is a combination for an Association Ad and Story Ad.

ASSOCIATION + STORY AD: PITCH

The following text combines many elements that use the fame of the author but try to overcome prejudice against his abilities as a fiction writer by invoking the fact that he is already a bestselling author, and by pitching the story of a world the author knows well. This is why references to Washington D.C. appear at the beginning and end of the text.

Example: *"The debut political thriller from Jake Tapper, CNN's chief Washington correspondent and the New York Times bestselling author of The Outpost—1950's D.C. intrigue about a secret society and a young Congressman in its grip."*

Elements breakdown:

"The debut"—Elements: fact, emotion (sense of discovery).

"Political thriller"—Elements: genre and style.

"Jake Tapper, CNN, New York Times bestselling author"—Elements: fact, association, success, objective authority.

"1950's D.C....grip"—Elements: story, genre.

CTA: CALL TO ACTION FORMATS

The goal of a call to action is to tell the recipients what you want them to do. The CTA can be part of the header or the text. There are various CTA styles that reflect how direct you want to be. Here are three variants of CTA.

1. **Suggestive** CTA—Example: *"Discover why so many readers are raving about this book!"*

2. **Hidden** CTA—Example: *"Mystery lovers are raving about this book!"*

3. **Command** CTA—Example: *"Get your own copy today!"*

CHAPTER 13

How to Deliver a Great Email Message to Foreign Publishers and Agents

E mail communication is, in our experience, the most cost–effective and flexible way to engage with your readers and pitch your book. Here is how you should break down the message elements and create an effective message.

OBJECTIVES

Keep your recipient in mind when you conceptualize the objective of your email. Do you want to make a sale? Do you want to inform? Do you want the recipient to be intrigued and look for more? Are they a new reader or already a fan of yours? Are you communicating to an agent or a publisher? Check out your Book ID. It will come in handy when making your message effective.

Your message should correlate to your Book ID and Book Passport, your target audience, and your objectives. As a writer, you have a way with words. Writing a compelling message shouldn't be a huge challenge. If you work within the framework of your campaign, the creative part should be a breeze. Your goal is to make the recipient want to do two things: first, read you message, and second, respond. We'll walk you through how to do this in this section and in upcoming sections that will be dedicated to the creative aspects of a successful campaign.

SUBJECT LINE

Incorporate your **hook** in the subject line. A 6–12–word hook should create an immediate impact with the recipient and draw them into the text.

Goal: Make the recipient want to open your email and read!

Examples:

- *"How did Joe Smith's new thriller become #1 in just two days?"*
- *"Your free copy for this amazing historical romance is just a click away!"*
- *"This is for you, because you like heartwarming cowboy romances…!"*

INSIDE HEADER

Use either your **logline** or a **review quote** as the header in your email. Be mindful not to repeat the header.

Goal: In 6–15 words, compose the essence of your message that leads to the main text.

Examples:

- *"A fierce young female detective stars in a new, exciting police series."*
- *"Dive into this dizzily shopaholic comedy!"*
- *"If this isn't the funniest book so far this year, it's up there!"*

SYNOPSIS/MAIN TEXT/RESUME

The main text should contain the synopsis. Use up to 150 words and include the USP and MUQ based on your Book ID and, if needed, your Book Passport. Include a short resume of the author and focus on information that supports your message.

Goal: Trigger the reader to want more without giving away too much, because that might have the exact opposite effect.

Examples:

- *"Neymar the Wizard is the fascinating coming-of-age story of Neymar da Silva Santos Junior, the skinny kid from Mogi das Cruzes, who has been called the next Pelé. Neymar has taken Brazil and the world by storm and inspired millions of fans around the world."*

- *"Following the international bestsellers,* The Flea— The Amazing Story of Leo Messi *and* Ronaldo—The Rise of a Winner, *author Michael Part brings home a heartwarming and emotional story of a father and son. Against all odds, they made the journey from the edge of poverty to international stardom through love, conviction, and a young boy's belief in himself."*

MHI–IMAGE/VIDEO

Goal: The MHI is the details that have to be included at the bottom of your message, such as the genre, age group, links to your social media platform, your contact information, and other crucial information. The image of your product, such as a 3D book cover or a flat .jpg, is a must. Other images, such as illustration or videos, could be great additions.

CHAPTER 14

How to Utilize Your Book as a Promotional Platform

YOUR BOOK'S TITLE

The most basic and powerful media platform is your book. From a marketing point of view, your book is a treasure trove. The four elements in play are the title, the cover, the inside pages, and the text itself. As mentioned before, always use the book as the major source.

The first major decision you should make is finding the right title. Choosing a title for most authors, especially for fiction books, is a very personal choice. It's either derived from an emotional bond or an artistic approach, or both, in which there is no consideration regarding the marketing value of the name. When authors choose a name and think about its marketing value, in many instances the decision isn't based on the Book ID or an analytical approach, in which case they may make wrong choices. From a marketing point of view, the title of a book is like any product name, and is the most important marketing element because it's always there and because it's the first thing the buyer comes in contact with. It is less important when the author brand is stronger than any of your individual books. But when your author brand is still in its infancy, the process of choosing the right title has to be methodical.

Answer the following questions:

1. Is the title based on the book ID? If the answer is no, move on.

2. Is the title free and clear? In most cases, you don't want to use a title that is already used. Do a title search first. See what titles are working in your category. This could help you determine if the title you need should be reminiscent of a successful title. Watch for patterns that work. How many words should be in the title? What is the style of the title?

3. Does the title stand out, and is it catchy?

4. How many message layers are in the title? Can you convey more than one message in the title? For example, *The Da Vinci Code* has multiple layers. It evokes feelings and images. It conveys history and art. The word "code" evokes mystery, riddles, detective work, and fiction based on true events. Four words with so much to say about the book. And the title has a straightforward connection to the story. It doesn't exist in limbo.

There are visible marketing elements, such as the cover, and some "hidden," those contained in the text itself.

COVER ELEMENTS

-   Main text: title, author's name.
-   Image and design.
-   Back–cover synopsis.
-   Spine text.
-   Other texts: quotes and blurbs from authors and critics, standings in the bestseller lists, and so on.

Creating the right cover isn't about having a pretty picture or design. Understanding that the cover is a major tool in your campaign will help you make the right decisions. You should look at the cover as an ad, or as a major part of an ad. A part of your campaign. It reflects your Book ID and the campaign's objectives.

Assuming that most of your marketing and sales efforts are done online, the size of your cover on the screen is pretty small. Keep in mind that the title of the book will appear separately from the cover itself in the ad's text and in the book page, so your focus should be on the image and the colors. For example, if you have a lot of white on the cover, it will morph with the screen. Many images are too small or have too many details to grasp. You have a split second to make an impact. Don't think pretty—think effective.

Because the cover is a constant, and you can't replace it like any other ad with fresh images, you should think in terms of long–term objectives. The composition of the elements should be dictated by the USP. For example, you should make your title the star of the cover if it has a strong promotional element in it. Your name should be the star if you are already a known commodity. If the book is a series, you want the design to be consistent with previous books, and if it's first in a series, then think about the next cover. If this is your first book, you should look for a great eye–catching image that brings out the genre right away. It's okay to look at the most successful books in your genre and adopt what worked for them.

You can mention your most successful book on the front cover, as well as the bestselling stature of this book, your other book, the series, and so on. You can also use the front cover for a very short review by a great objective authority. All of the above applies to the back cover, where you usually place the synopsis, the "About the Author" section, and so on. This isn't important with an eBook, so you might consider having elements that are traditionally on the back cover appear on the front. For example, your social media links.

MAKING THE MOST OF THE BACK–COVER TEXT

For a printed book in a brick and mortar book store, the back–cover text can make a whole lot of difference. On an eBook, it doesn't have any value. Still it's important to have a back–cover text because it can serve as a great post, and it works in the book's product page, as well as ads, press releases, and marketing emails. Writing a great back–cover text is vital because it is an opportunity to present, in 100–150 words, a microcosm of your book as an art form and product.

A great back–cover text reflects the essence of the book. It could be a short excerpt from the book, or all the four ad prototypes combined. But be careful not to cross the line and make it look like an ad.

In your eBook, place the back–cover synopsis at the beginning of the book, right after the front cover, before the copyright page.

CHAPTER 15

How to Reach Readers and Build a Following

Reaching out to your first reader is the hardest thing in this phase of your journey. We tend to look beyond our close circle of family and friends in search of a random reader. No doubt this should be your ultimate goal, and having readers from the general public buying and reading your book is a worthwhile goal. When that moment arrives, you should be ready to make that reader not only your book's reader, but *your* reader. Your fan.

But before that happens, you should focus on building your readership from the bottom up. If you are one of the many authors who published your book by crowdfunding, you probably did just that by tapping into your closest circle of family and friends to complete the publishing phase, thereby reaching your first group of readers. That is precisely where you ought to look. Going directly to the general public might be costly. So, don't overlook your immediate circle. This is where you should begin your journey.

ASSEMBLING READERS' DATA

Get started by assembling a potential readers list made up of your family, friends, acquaintances, and colleagues. If you are signed up to multiple platforms like Facebook, LinkedIn, Twitter, and Instagram, compiling these lists and reaching out to these people should be fairly easy.

Begin with segmenting groups from your immediate circle, and rate how interested they might be in your book and what role they might play in assisting you. First, rank people most likely to show interest in your book and respond in a timely manner to your outreach. Split them into these categories:

1. Family and friends who are avid readers.
2. Friends and their friends who have interest in books and genres similar to yours. You can track their interests by looking closely into their Facebook pages.
3. Fellow self–published authors that you know.

Rate these groups with the following traits in mind:

- Those most likely to write a favorable review or blurb.
- Those most likely to post and share your messages, emails, and posts.
- Those most likely to assist in organizing live events, such as reading groups.
- Those most likely to become loyal readers interested in your future books.

These readers will form the bedrock of your fanbase. Start with five, twenty, or fifty readers. They are your most valuable readers, essential to your success, and you need to treat them as such.

REACHING OUT TO INFLUENCERS

Next are the influencers. Some of them can be found in your first circle, others you should identify outside it. They include bloggers, YouTubers, professionals, and traditional journalists who might have an interest in your book because of the subject matter or your personal story. Nonfiction books are easier to define. If your subject matter could be of interest to a certain segment of the public, or fellow professionals, targeting and pitching could be easier. Build a list of influencers, bloggers, and print, TV, and radio journalists. Find an angle or a storyline that could stand out as a news item, and make a solid pitch.

TARGETING YOUR READERS

Targeting starts at creating the lists we discussed before. Friends, acquaintances, neighbors, colleagues, and so on. Each group should have a targeted profile. The same applies to the second and third circles—the people you don't know.

Targeting is an art of trial and error. This is the process where you should figure out whom your readers or potential buyers are and build profiles that are as detailed as possible.

This is our method of building a targeted audience profile:

1. Divide profiles into readers and customers. As discussed earlier, they are sometimes not the same.

2. Write down as many details as you can about the profile.
   - General details such as: interest, gender, age, location, education, occupation, family, income, and so on.
   - What are their literary interests such as fiction, nonfiction, favorite genre, and so on?
   - How many books do they read over a period of a year?
   - Are they fans of other authors or series?
   - What are their social media preferences?
   - Are they eBook readers or print readers?

   Having a detailed profile will help you in your digital social media efforts in defining the audience, the platform, and the creative.

3. Once you have a general profile, you can build multiple audiences that are narrow and specific. For example, in

marketing a children's book about Sir Alex Ferguson, the legendary Manchester United manager, we started with Manchester United fans all over the world. Next, we only included fans who love children's books, or those who have teen kids and are interested in books, and then we narrowed the locality to the UK or to the city of Manchester, England.

We began this process by starting with as big and as general an audience that would relate to the book, and by narrowing, excluding, and refining the audience we got from 120 million to 500,000 or less. Once you get your first audience, you'll be able to create many more audiences by changing variables. By trial and error, you'll find what audiences work best.

The process of targeting is based on your profiles. You can create dozens of audiences. Some will yield disappointing results, and some will shine.

4. Targeting starts with configuring your Book ID, but when you go further, and you create multiple campaigns and ads, the general definitions won't be sufficient. Even having a good number of audiences isn't enough. You should match your audience to the campaign objectives. So first ask yourself what your goal in a specific ad is, then create the best ads and match then with the right audience.

5. Always make the connection between objective and results when judging your choice of targeting. And give it time. Testing over time might give you great insight into your target audiences. Their response will give you a better idea of what worked and what didn't. Understanding results is vital. You might get great responses for an ad and you still won't get any sales. Was your targeting accurate? Depends on your objective. If your objective was to scratch the surface, get people a first glimpse without converting them into buyers, you've done great. If your goal was to get

sales, your choice of audience was wrong. Still, some audiences need more time. You should expose them to your ad multiple times to make then act. You might have targeted your audience correctly, but you didn't have patience to wait for results. Targeting is complex. Being patient is vital. You'll learn a lot from your audiences' responses. Study the analytics. Fine tune. Try again. And again.

DEEP TARGETING

When we buy a book, we don't purchase just a "product," a special price, or features; we purchase an experience. Everything we buy in life has an emotional reason behind it, and with books, interest and emotions go hand in hand.

In order to meet readers' needs, you must dig deeper and start testing different emotional triggers to identify how to communicate with your readers.

Digital marketing is moving further from mass reach and segmentation targeting to targeting based on emotions and behavioral patterns.

How does this apply to you? You won't have the big data that Netflix, Amazon, or Facebook have, but you can learn a lot from your readers' social media activity, from reviews, and from an ongoing dialogue with your readers.

Communicating with your readers can tell you a lot about them. Offer your readers to write to you, or fill in a questionnaire, or join your group. Read their reviews and their comments. You'll understand how to approach them, and their words will become the building blocks of your future messages.

There are marketing professionals who think that geography and age are things of the past. They are targeting audiences based exclusively on their content choices. You have to do the same in your own little world with much simpler yet useful means. Even reading reviews for books in your category can teach you a lot about your readers.

MAKING A SALE ONE COPY AT A TIME

Making a sale is the ultimate goal, and it will be your most challenging effort after the book is published. It's not just a legitimate business goal, it's a validation of your work. It is especially gratifying when it comes from strangers. There are people out there who are intrigued by your work, and they responded to your CTA and made a purchase. Hopefully, they'll recommend the book to others.

Making a sale requires you to plan for the short, medium, and long haul. Pay attention to the following:

1. Make sales projections: The minimum number of copies you would like to sell in the first year, how many you expect to sell to your first circle, and how many you expect to sell to the broader public.
2. Make a budget: The amount of money you are willing to invest in selling the minimum number of copies.
3. Plan and execute a lean and flexible marketing and distribution plan.
4. Create sales platforms: Establish your presence on the various bookselling platforms, and learn how to maximize your sales through each platform.
5. Own media rights: Sell rights, whether to other media, like TV, movies, games, and so on, or sell translation rights.

These are all interconnected. Once you have configured the Book ID/Passport, the Reader ID, the Author ID, and laid the ground for your first circle of readers, you will have all the elements in place to move to the next phase of making a sale. This is a crucial step in the process, in which each decision is critical to your success. But these decisions can be fixed, so if you make mistakes—and who doesn't?—you can correct them. It's a process. You can't expect to get results overnight. And you have time to assess what you have accomplished, and make changes.

Being a micropublisher requires time and money. You can't expect to only spend resources on producing the book. The exchange is clear: The more you do it yourself, the less money you'll spend, and the more control you'll retain. At each step of the way, you might find yourself in a position in which you decide to buy assistance and expertise in areas you feel you need them. *But you should do this wisely and make sure that there is correlation between investment and success.* You should always be in control, which means that you know exactly what you need, and how to evaluate what you get in return for your investment.

BUILDING YOUR CAMPAIGNS FROM THE BOTTOM UP

The exciting news that yet another book was born might be thrilling to a very limited group of people. Oftentimes, it feels very lonely when your book makes its first steps in the world, and after a week or two, or even a month, you feel as if you and your book were left alone, unnoticed and uncared for.

Don't let yourself sink into despair. There are so many things you can do to make your book relevant, alive, and in demand. It's your *duty* to give your book a shot.

That is exactly why you must define your campaign goals and implementation timeline. As mentioned previously, you can begin from the very early stages of the writing process, or when the book is ready. The point is, by planning, you are not only creating a system; you are using your time and resources more efficiently.

Goal #1: Reaching readers and building awareness. If your goal is to engage a significant number of loyal readers, regardless of how many books you sell, and build a name for yourself and your book, your campaign should target avid readers, book bloggers, and YouTubers—people who love to read and can spread the word within your close circle and in the wider world.

Because these are very busy people with a lot of books on their reading lists, don't be deterred if you don't get an immediate response. Don't expect people to leave everything they do and grab your book the moment they hear about it. Engage them. Send your pitches in intervals. Let them know about you and your book before they even read the first page. *Turn them into your fans first, and your readers later.* Your style of communication might make or break your success. Don't *sell* to these people—try to capture their attention!

Goal #2: Sell as many copies as you can. You can always combine the two goals. But if your main goal is to sell, you need to define a timetable in which you split your time between two separate periods:

Trial period: During this time, you'll do your own A/B testing. "Manually" test dozens of mini ad campaigns, and define your exact target audience. Give yourself at least a month for this prelaunch phase.

Launch phase: During this time, you'll begin both paid and free social media campaigns to try to convert your close circle, and later the wider public, into customers. Save the giveaways for strangers. Get the sales from your friends and acquaintances. When you reach out to people you don't know, a giveaway of a book in return for their email address is a great investment. The earnings from your closer circle will come in handy when you begin your paid campaigns.

WORDWIDE AND AFTER PUBLISHING

We hope this book gave you beneficial inputs as to the post–publishing phase. Aside from our ongoing work via Sole Books, we are assisting self–published authors and micropublishers in getting their books to the world via our WordWide service.

At After Publishing, we are developing a series of services and features that will assist you in creating book marketing campaigns at ease. If you are interested in learning more, join our mailing list at *info@afterpublishing.com*.